365
DAYS OF
THANKING
GOD

OTHER BOOKS
by Daniella Whyte

The Girl God Wants:
Sister-to-Sister Talk on Loving God,
Living a Great Life, and Enjoying It

The Thanksgiving That Almost Wasn't

Letters to All Young Women
(co-authored)

Dear Papa: Letters to My Father
(co-authored)

365 DAYS OF THANKING GOD

CULTIVATING A HEART OF EVERYDAY THANKS

Compiled and Edited by
Daniella Whyte

365 Days of Thanking God:
Cultivating a Heart of Everyday Thanks

Cover Design by Atinad Designs

TORCH LEGACY PUBLICATIONS, DALLAS, TEXAS;
ATLANTA, GEORGIA; BROOKLYN, NEW YORK

First Printing, 2010

The Bible quotations in this volume are from the King James Version of the Bible.

The name TORCH LEGACY PUBLICATIONS and its logo are registered as a trademark in the U.S. patent office.

ISBN-13: 978-0-9830141-1-9

Printed in the U.S.A.

This book is dedicated to God.
I am thankful for the life You have given me.

To my father who is thankful for everything and
who taught me to be the same.

INTRODUCTION

Thanksgiving has always been my favorite time of the year. Not only do I love the season, but I love the holiday spirit that fills people and the change of pace that takes place during this season. I look forward to this time of the year every year. Thanksgiving is also very special to me because I was born on this day nineteen years ago. Besides that, my family also celebrates the Thanksgiving holiday in a big way.

As the years have passed and one Thanksgiving after another has come and gone, I have begun to think about why Thanksgiving has been reserved to one day out of the year. I began to wonder why many people don't take the time to count the blessings of each day. As I pondered this question, I came to the realization that millions of people go through their life searching for the next big thing and trying to be the biggest or the best at everything, that they do not take the time to be thankful for the small, everyday blessings that God gives in life. If we would take the time to step aside each day and count the blessings that God has bestowed upon us, in His mercy and grace, I think we would be a much happier people.

The attitude and spirit of ungratefulness exists in every facet of life. Thousands of men and women are not thankful for the way God made them, so they try to change their physical features to try to make themselves more appealing to the world. Many young people are not thankful for the life and energy that God has given them, so they whittle away their time with slothfulness, purposelessness, and foolishness. Still many more people are not thankful for their positions in life so they try to move or change their position to what they think is better for them. I have been in grocery store lines where cashiers and customers do not say "thank you" to each other. Even some Christians are so busy trying to get to the "next level" or get to their "destiny" in life that they do not take the time to thank God for the place where He has them right now.

Many husbands and wives are not thankful for each other so they get divorced. Many children are not thankful for their parents so they rebel. Many students are not thankful for the opportunity to gain knowledge so they disrespect their teachers. Many governmental officials and authority figures in our communities are not thankful for the office that has been given to them, so they abuse it. Some pastors are not thankful for the flock that has been committed to their stewardship, so they take the money of the congregation and use the people's troubles for personal gain.

How difficult it must be for God to continue to bless a people who are so ungrateful? What if He decided to stop blessing this world? What if He chose to stop holding up the world in the palm of His hand? What if He didn't love His creation anymore and decided to pull back His life-giving hand from our bodies? We should be thankful that God is a longsuffering and compassionate God Who keeps on blessing us inspite of our ungratefulness.

I have come to realize that unthankfulness stems from a heart of pride. I say that because many people think that they are all powerful and that all they have and all they have accomplished is because of them and their hard work. Many of us feel as though we deserve what we have. We feel entitled to the good things that come to us and that we are too perfect for anything bad to happen to us. These are false notions of sinful human nature.

We should be humble and realize that everyday we live, and every good thing we do, is because of God's grace at work in the earth. I have realized that whatever good comes to me, comes from God, whatever bad comes to me, God has allowed it, and I choose to be thankful for both.

This book is not about the holiday called Thanksgiving. It is not about how to celebrate Thanksgiving. This book is a challenge to you to cultivate a heart of thankfulness to God and to the people He has placed in your life.

Contained in this book are 122 things that I thank God for, 122 Bible verses on being thankful, and 122 quotations about thankfulness. Thankfulness is not about keeping a tradition. It is a matter of the heart. It should be an everyday occurence. It should be a habit; it should be a way of life. It may seem as though it is small or insignificant to you, but it means a lot to God and to others. I pray that this book will encourage you and challenge you to be thankful for everything.

Daniella Whyte

Dallas, TX

GIVING THANKS ALWAYS FOR ALL
THINGS UNTO GOD AND THE FATHER IN
THE NAME OF OUR LORD JESUS CHRIST.

Ephesians 5:20

YOU SIMPLY WILL NOT BE THE SAME

PERSON TWO MONTHS FROM NOW

AFTER CONSCIOUSLY GIVING THANKS

EACH DAY FOR THE ABUNDANCE THAT

EXISTS IN YOUR LIFE. AND YOU WILL

HAVE SET IN MOTION AN ANCIENT

SPIRITUAL LAW: THE MORE YOU HAVE

AND ARE GRATEFUL FOR, THE MORE

WILL BE GIVEN YOU.

SARAH BAN BREATHNACH

3 REASONS TO BE THANKFUL

God expects thanksgiving from His creation.

Psalm 100:4 says, *"Enter into His gates with thanksgiving..."* What kind of God would God be if He kept on blessing us, but He did not expect some praise in return? When we thank God for things He does for us everyday, He appreciates that. You might be saying, 'Well, I don't have a job' or 'My family is in trouble' or 'Someone close to me is seriously ill.' God understands all of that because He knew where you would be and what you would be doing right now before you were even born. The point is, inspite of everything else that is going on in our lives, if we are alive, we need to be thanking God.

Not only does God expect thankfulness, but human beings react differently to thankful people. If you do something for someone and he or she does not show appreciation to you, will you be more or less eager to do something else for that person the next time around? Thankfulness is a very simple concept; it is very elementary. Being thankful not only shows good manners, but a simple expression of thankfulness can go a long way. It makes other people feel wanted and appreciated and it can enhance our relationships.

**We feel better about ourselves
if we exhibit thankfulness.**

Not only does God expect our thankfulness and praise and not only do other people appreciate our thankful attitude, but on the inside, we feel better about ourselves if we exhibit a thankful attitude and behaviour. Thankfulness is not just about words because words can be said without meaning.

Thankfulness is about heart because everything that is done from the heart is sincere. Many of us can ask for what we want and oftentimes will get it. But if we are not truly thankful from the heart for what we already have, then we block our opportunities to obtain more.

I believe that contentment in life begins with having a thankful heart. Things change when we exhibit thankfulness and mean it. So, may I encourage you to let yourself be reminded of all the good (and the bad) things that have happened in your life. As an old hymn says, "Count them one by one." And you will soon realize that even if you aren't rich, even if you're not in the best situation, even if you aren't popular or powerful, you and I have a lot to be thankful for.

A CHALLENGE TO BE THANKFUL

Everyday, think of one thing to thank God for, read a quote on being thankful, or read a verse from the Bible on thankfulness. For 365 days, do one of these three things. The Bible tells us to give thanks always; not just when we feel like it or when everything is going well. King David commanded the children of Israel in 1 Chronicles 23:30 to *"stand every morning to thank and praise the Lord, and likewise at even."* This is a great way to start and end your day. By choosing to be thankful for at least one thing a day, you will begin to cultivate a heart of continual thankfulness.

God bless!

DAY 1

I am thankful for salvation
through Jesus Christ.

DAY 2

"We have received too much from God to allow
ourselves opportunities for unbelief. We have
received too many gifts and privileges to allow a
grumbling, murmuring heart to disqualify us of
our destiny. In contrast, the thankful heart sees the
best part of every situation. It sees problems and
weaknesses as opportunities, struggles as refining
tools, and sinners as saints in progress."
FRANCIS FRANGIPANE

DAY 3

"Enter into His gates with thanksgiving,
and into His courts with praise:
be thankful unto Him and bless His name."
PSALM 100:4

DAY 4

I am thankful for the hope of Heaven.

DAY 5

"Remember that not to be happy
is not to be grateful."
ELIZABETH CARTER

DAY 6

"O give thanks unto the Lord; call upon
His name: make known His deeds among
the people."
PSALM 105:1

DAY 7

I am thankful for
God's faithfulness.

DAY 8

"When the Christian praises and gives thanks to God, this not only pleases God, but it enriches the Christian's life with joy. It is a reciprocating transaction between God and man."
RICK WARREN

DAY 9

"Offer unto God thanksgiving; and pay thy vow unto the Most High."
PSALM 50:14

I am thankful for
the love of God.

DAY 11

"Jesus is moved to happiness every time He sees that you appreciate what He has done for you. Grip His pierced hand and say to Him, 'I thank Thee, Saviour, because Thou has died for me.' Thank Him likewise for all the other blessings He has showered upon you from day to day. It brings joy to Jesus."
OLE KRISTIAN O. HALLESBY

DAY 12

"In everything give thanks: for this is the will of God in Christ Jesus concerning you."
I THESSALONIANS 5:18

I am thankful for the freedom
to do what is right.

"Happiness is impossible without gratitude."
DENNIS PRAGER

"Rooted and built up in Him, and stablished in
the faith, as ye have been taught, abounding
therein with thanksgiving."
COLOSSIANS 2:7

I am thankful for the sacrifice
of Jesus Christ.

DAY 17

"It is a rare person who, when his cup
frequently runs over, can thank God instead of
complaining about the limited size of his mug!"
BOB RUSSELL

DAY 18

"Praise ye the Lord. O give thanks unto the
Lord; for He is good: for His mercy
endureth for ever."
PSALM 106:1

I am thankful for the power of prayer and the power of praying people.

"Thanksgiving is good,
but 'thanksliving' is better."
SELECTED

"And He took the cup and gave thanks, and gave it unto them, saying, Drink ye all of it."
MATTHEW 26:27

I am thankful that God is always in control of everything.

"Learn the lesson of thanksgiving. It is due to God, it is due to ourselves. Thanksgiving for the past makes us trustful in the present and hopeful for the future. What He has done is the pledge of what He will do."
A. C. A. HALL

"Then they took away the stone from the place where the dead was laid. And Jesus lifted up His eyes, and said, Father, I thank thee that thou hast heard Me."
JOHN 11:41

I am thankful for life.

DAY 26

"I asked for strength, and God gave me difficulties to make me strong. I asked for wisdom, and God gave me problems to solve. I asked for prosperity, and God gave me brain and brawn to work. I asked for courage, and God gave me dangers to overcome. I asked for love, and God gave me opportunities. I received nothing I wanted, I received everything I needed. My prayer has been answered."

MICHAEL JOB

DAY 27

"And when those beasts give glory and honour and thanks to Him that sat on the throne, who liveth for ever and ever, The four and twenty elders fall down before him that sat on the throne, and worship him that liveth for ever and ever, and cast their crowns before the throne."

REVELATION 4:9-10

I am thankful that God has counted me worthy by putting me into the ministry.

"The careless soul receives the Father's gifts as if it were a way things had of dropping into his hand... yet he is ever complaining, as if someone were accountable for the problems which meet him at every turn. For the good that comes to him, he gives no thanks—who is there to thank? At the disappointments that befall him he grumbles— there must be someone to blame!"
GEORGE MACDONALD

"And I thank Christ Jesus our Lord, who hath enabled me, for that He counted me faithful, putting me into the ministry."
I TIMOTHY 1:12

I am thankful for peace that passeth all understanding.

"The failure to return thanks for definite blessings received is a manifestation of ingratitude that grieves Jesus Christ."
R. A. TORREY

"And I thank Christ Jesus our Lord, who hath enabled me, for that He counted me faithful, putting me into the ministry."
I TIMOTHY 1:12

I am thankful for good health.

DAY 35

"Being thankful is not telling God you appreciate the fact that your life is not in shambles. If that is the basis of your gratitude, you are on slippery ground. Every day of your life you face the possibility that a blessing in your life may be taken away. But blessings are only signs of God's love. The real blessing, of course, is the love itself...We are not ultimately grateful that we are still holding our blessings. We are grateful that we are held by God even when the blessings are slipping through our fingers."
CRAIG BARNES

DAY 36

"I will sing unto the Lord because He hath dealt bountifully with me."
PSALM 13:6

I am thankful for music.

"Nothing is more honorable
than a grateful heart."
SHAKESPEARE

"First, I thank my God through Jesus Christ for
you all, that your faith is spoken of throughout
the whole world."
ROMANS 1:8

I am thankful for sunshine.

"The best things are nearest: breath in your nostrils, light in your eyes, flowers at your feet, duties at your hand, the path of God just before you."
ROBERT LOUIS STEVENSON

"Whoso offereth praise glorifieth me: and to him that ordereth his conversation aright will I shew the salvation of God."
PSALMS 50:23

I am thankful for purpose
in life.

"You say, 'If I had a little more, I should be very
satisfied.' You make a mistake. If you are not
content with what you have, you would not be
satisfied if it were doubled."
CHARLES HADDON SPURGEON

"Giving thanks always for all things unto God
and the Father in the name of our
Lord Jesus Christ."
EPHESIANS 5:20

I am thankful for a loving family.

"The soul must forget about understanding, and abandon itself into the arms of love, and His Majesty will teach it what to do next; almost its whole work is to realize its unworthiness to receive such great good and to occupy itself in thanksgiving."
TERESA OF AVILA

"By Him therefore let us offer the sacrifice of praise to God continually, that is, the fruit of our lips giving thanks to His name."
HEBREWS 13:15

I am thankful for the death, burial, and resurrection of Jesus Christ.

"Too many of us are low-voiced and shallow-streamed in our gratitude."
SELECTED

"Ye also helping together by prayer for us, that for the gift bestowed upon us by the means of many persons thanks may be given by many on our behalf."
II CORINTHIANS 1:11

I am thankful for the holiday
and the spirit of
Thanksgiving.

DAY 53

"God is glorified, not by our groans,
but by our thanksgivings."
ANONYMOUS

DAY 54

"Now when Daniel knew that the writing was
signed, he went into his house; and his
windows being open in his chamber toward
Jerusalem, he kneeled upon his knees three
times a day, and prayed, and gave thanks before
his God, as he did aforetime."
DANIEL 6:10

I am thankful for shelter.

"Every virtue divorced from thankfulness is
maimed and limps along the spiritual road."
HENRY WARD BEECHER

"I will give Thee thanks in the great
congregation: I will praise Thee among
much people."
PSALM 35:18

DAY 58

I am thankful for the gifts God
has given me.

DAY 59

"Because we cannot see just what God is saving
us from, we vent our foolish reproaches; if we
could see this, we would often kneel down and
thank God for certain trials as the richest of His
mercies."
SELECTED

DAY 60

"We give thanks to God always for you all,
making mention of you in our prayers."
I THESSALONIANS 1:2

I am thankful for wisdom.

"God is a great giver, let us be great
in giving thanks."
SELECTED

"And Jesus took the loaves; and when
He had given thanks, He distributed to the
disciples, and the disciples to them that were
set down; and like wise of the fishes
as much as they would."
JOHN 6:11

I am thankful for my pastor.

"We ought to give thanks for all fortune: if it is 'good,' because is it good, if 'bad' because it works in us patience, humility, and the contempt of this world and the hope of our eternal country."
C. S. LEWIS

"And when He had thus spoken,
He took bread, and gave thanks to God
in the presence of them all: and when
He had broken it, He began to eat."
ACTS 27:35

I am thankful for the rain.

"Let the thankful heart sweep through the day
and, as the magnet finds the iron, so it will find,
in every hour, some heavenly blessings."
HENRY WARD BEECHER

"Wherefore I also, after I heard of your faith in
the Lord Jesus, and love unto all the saints,
Cease not to give thanks for you, making
mention of you in my prayers."
EPHESIANS 1:15-16

I am thankful for the
storms of life.

"In the old Anglo-Saxon, to be 'thankful' meant
to be 'thinkful.' Thinking of one's blessings
should stir one to gratitude."
UNKNOWN

"Sing unto the Lord, O ye saints of His,
and give thanks at the remembrance
of His holiness."
PSALM 30:4

I am thankful for
a good heart.

"Being infinitely amazed, so do I give thanks
to God, Who has been pleased to make me the
first observer of marvelous things,
unrevealed to bygone ages."
GALILEO

"Rejoice in the Lord, ye righteous; and give
thanks at the remembrance of His holiness."
PSALM 97:12

I am thankful for humility.

"While I would fain have some tincture of all the virtues, there is no quality I would rather have, and be thought to have, than gratitude. For it is not only the greatest virtue, but even the mother of all the rest."

CICERO

"O give thanks unto the Lord, for He is good; for His mercy endureth for ever."

PSALM 107:1

I am thankful for the ability
to help others.

"God never promises to remove us from our struggles. He does promise, however, to change the way we look at them."
Max Lucado

"Thanks be unto God for His unspeakable gift."
II Corinthians 9:15

I am thankful for
understanding people.

"If we pause to think,
we'll have cause to thank."
SELECTED

"We give Thee thanks, O Lord God
Almighty, which art, and wast, and art, to come:
because Thou hast taken to Thee thy great
power, and hast reigned."
REVELATION 11:17

DAY 85

I am thankful for the
ability to love.

DAY 86

"Gratitude... goes beyond the 'mine' and 'thine' and claims the truth that all of life is a pure gift. In the past I always thought of gratitude as a spontaneous response to the awareness of gifts received, but now I realize that gratitude can also be lived as a discipline. The discipline of gratitude is the explicit effort to acknowledge that all I am and have is given to me as a gift of love, a gift to be celebrated with joy."

HENRI J. M. NOUWEN

DAY 87

"For this cause also, thank we God without ceasing, because, when ye received the word of God which ye heard of us, ye received it not as the word of men, but as it is in truth, the word of God, which effectually worketh also in you that believe."

I THESSALONIANS 2:13

DAY 88

I am thankful that life is not always smooth sailing and that some roses have thorns.

DAY 89

"Begin by thanking Him for some little thing, and then go on, day by day, adding to your subjects of praise; thus you will find their numbers grow wonderfully; and, in the same proportion, will your subjects of murmuring and complaining diminish, until you see in everything some cause for thanksgiving."
PRISCILLA MAURICE

DAY 90

"I thank God through Jesus Christ our Lord. So then with the mind I myself serve the law of God; but with the flesh the law of sin."
ROMANS 7:25

I am thankful that God has made every person unique and spec al.

"Gratitude is the least of the virtues, but ingratitude is the worst of vices."
Thomas Fuller

"But thanks be to God which giveth us the victory through our Lord Jesus Christ."
I Corinthians 15:57

DAY 94

I am thankful that I am not
rich.

DAY 95

"A heart that does not have the true ability to be
utterly and genuinely delighted and grateful at
the simple gift given by a friend, will find it
equally as difficult to be utterly delighted in the
gifts given by the King."
KATHERINE WALDEN

DAY 96

"I thank Thee, and praise Thee, O thou God of
my fathers, who hast given me wisdom and
might, and hast made known unto me now
what we desired of Thee; for Thou hast now
made known unto us the king's matter."
DANIEL 2:23

DAY 97

I am thankful for
encouragement.

DAY 98

"Thanksgiving is a duty before it's a feeling."
SELECTED

DAY 99

"Now thanks be unto God, which always
causeth us to triumph in Christ, and maketh
manifest the savour of His knowledge by us
in every place."
II CORINTHIANS 2:14

I am thankful for rebuke.

"Thanks begins with the thankful.
It is not dependent upon anyone else.
Speak it. Give it. Live it."
WILLIAM O. VICKERY

"But God be thanked, that ye were the servants
of sin, but ye have obeyed from the heart that
form of doctrine which was delivered you."
ROMANS 6:17

I am thankful for unbroken
promises.

"Though my mouth be dumb,
my heart shall thank you."
NICHOLAS ROWE

"And they lifted up their voices, and said, Jesus, Master,
have mercy on us. And when he saw them, he said unto
them, Go shew yourselves unto the priests. And it came to
pass, that, as they went, they were cleansed. And one of
them, when he saw that he was healed, turned back, and
with a loud voice glorified God, And fell down on his face
at His feet, giving Him thanks: and he was a Samaritan."
LUKE 17:13-16

I am thankful for food to eat.

"Thanksgiving is a recognition of a debt that cannot be paid. We express thanks, whether or not we are able otherwise to reimburse the giver. When thanksgiving is filled with true meaning and is not just the formality of a polite 'thank you,' it is the recognition of dependence."
BILLY GRAHAM

"We are bound to thank God always for you, brethren, as it is meet, because that your faith groweth exceedingly, and the charity of every one of you all toward each other aboundeth."
II THESSALONIANS 1:3

DAY 109

I am thankful that I know that having a good heart is the most important thing, and looks and material things are not.

DAY 110

"In spite of the many benefits God has blessed us with, how many times do we complain about little difficulties and trials? We lose sight of the big picture and fail to appreciate the really important things. Just as we cannot benefit from a wrapped gift under a Christmas tree until we open it, so gratitude can be seen as our way of opening the gift of God's love intended by all the small and big positive events of our lives."
RONDA DE SOLA CHERVIN

DAY 111

"I thank my God always on your behalf, for the grace of God which is given you by Jesus Christ."
I CORINTHIANS 1:4

I am thankful for faith.

"From a heart overflowing with gratitude, we will want to honour and glorify God by gratefully offering back to Him the many good gifts He has bestowed on us. We will not go to church to be entertained, to see 'what we can get out of it' for our own private gratification, but rather to praise and worship the triune God of grace and glory."

ANONYMOUS

"I thank my God upon every remembrance of you."

PHILIPPIANS 1:3

I am thankful that every day is
a new day, full of wonder,
grace, and opportunity.

"A thankful heart enjoys blessings twice—
when they're received,
and when they're remembered."
SELECTED

"We give thanks to God and the Father of our
Lord Jesus Christ, praying always for you."
COLOSSIANS 1:3

DAY 118

I am thankful for America.

DAY 119

"Ingratitude is always a form of weakness.
I have never known a man of real ability
to be ungrateful."
GOETHE

DAY 120

"But thanks be to God, which put the same
earnest care into the heart of Titus for you."
II CORINTHIANS 8:16

DAY 121

I am thankful that life is not
about me.

DAY 122

"A thankful heart is not only the greatest virtue,
but the parent of all other values."
CICERO

DAY 123

"Unto Thee O God, do we give thanks, unto
Thee do we give thanks: for that Thy name is
near Thy wondrous works declare."
PSALM 75:1

I am thankful to be on
mission with God.

"All our discontents spring from the want of
thankfulness for what we have."
DANIEL DEFOE

"Now therefore, our God, we thank Thee, and
praise Thy glorious name."
II CHRONICLES 29:13

DAY 127

I am thankful that seasons of life change.

DAY 128

"It is easy to be thankful when we remember just how totally dependent upon God we are."
MAIN ST. MONITOR

DAY 129

"He that regardeth the day, regardeth it unto the Lord; and he that regardeth not the day, to the Lord he doth not regard it. He that eateth, eateth to the Lord, for he giveth God thanks; and he that eateth not, to the Lord he eateth not, and giveth God thanks."
ROMANS 14:6

I am thankful for the promises
of God in the Bible.

DAY 131

"Cultivate a thankful spirit! It will be to thee a
perpetual feast. There is, or ought to be, with us
no such thing as small mercies; all are great,
because the least are undeserved. Indeed a really
thankful heart will extract motive for gratitude
from everything, making the most even of
scanty blessings."
J. R. MacDuff

DAY 132

"For every creature of God is good,
and nothing to be refused, if it be received
with thanksgiving."
I Timothy 4:4

I am thankful for a
friendly spirit.

"I imagine that it saddens the heart of God
when we murmur and complain, instead of
being thankful after He's been so good to us."
JOYCE MEYER

"I exhort therefore, that, first of all,
supplications, prayers, intercessions and giving
of thanks, be made for all men."
I TIMOTHY 2:1

I am thankful for a
good education.

"Gratitude shouldn't be an occasional incident
but a continuous attitude."
SELECTED

"Being enriched in every thing to all
bountifulness, which causeth through us
thanksgiving to God."
II CORINTHIANS 9:11

DAY 139

I am thankful that Jesus Christ paves the way for us each day.

DAY 140

"Gratitude as a discipline involves a conscious choice. I can choose to be grateful even when my emotions and feelings are still steeped in hurt and resentment. It is amazing how many occasions present themselves in which I can choose gratitude instead of a complaint. I can choose to be grateful when I am criticized, even when my heart still responds in bitterness. I can choose to speak about goodness and beauty, even when my inner eye still looks for someone to accuse or something to call ugly."
Henri J. M. Nouwen

DAY 141

"I thank God, whom I serve from my forefathers with pure conscience, that without ceasing I have remembrance of thee in my prayers night and day."
II Timothy 1:3

DAY 142

I am thankful even for
sickness.

DAY 143

"The unthankful heart discovers no mercies;
but the thankful heart will find, in every hour,
some heavenly blessings."
HENRY WARD BEECHER

DAY 144

"It is good for me that I have been afflicted; that
I might learn thy statutes."
PSALM 119:71

I am thankful for strength.

"The hardest arithmetic to master is that which
enables us to count our blessings."
ERIC HOFFER

"Be careful for nothing, but in everything by
prayer and supplication with thanksgiving let
your requests be made known unto God."
PHILIPPIANS 4:6

I am thankful for Saturdays, Sundays, Mondays, Tuesdays, Wednesdays, Thursdays, and FRIDAYS.

"We need deliberately to call to mind the joys of our journey. Perhaps we should try to write down the blessings of one day. We might begin; we could never end; there are not pens or paper enough in all the world."
GEORGE A. BUTTRICK

"Continue in prayer and watch in the same with thanksgiving."
COLOSSIANS 4:2

I am thankful for God's grace.

On the night I was robbed: "I thanked the Lord first because I was never robbed before; second, because although they took my purse they did not take my life; third, although they took my all, it was not much; and fourth, because it was I who was robbed and not I who robbed."
MATTHEW HENRY

"It is a good thing to give thanks unto the Lord,
and to sing praises unto Thy name,
O Most High."
PSALM 92:1

I am thankful that one day, at
a set time, I will go to Heaven
to be with the Lord.

"That thing that is not coming to you may seem good.
But either the timing is wrong, or from His position
He can see that the future of it is bleak. I have always
believed that people who thank God only for
delivering them from what happened are just scraping
the surface of praise. The real praise comes when you
start thanking Him for what could have happened but
didn't because of His swift grace!"
T. D. JAKES

"And let the peace of God rule in your hearts,
to the which also ye are called in one body;
and be ye thankful."
COLOSSIANS 3:15

I am thankful for the occasional embarrassment because every once in a while, we need to be humbled.

"How many times do we miss God's blessings because they are not packaged as we expected?"
ANONYMOUS

"And she coming in that instant gave thanks likewise unto the Lord, and spake of Him to all them who looked for redemption in Jerusalem."
LUKE 2:38

I am thankful
for thankful people.

"The most important prayer in the world is just
two words long: 'Thank you.'"
MEISTER ECKHART

"I will offer to Thee the sacrifice of
thanksgiving, and will call upon the name
of the Lord."
PSALM 116:17

I am thankful that I have a
purpose in life.

"Oh what a happy soul am I although I cannot
see, I am resolved that in this world contented I
shall be. How many blessings I enjoy that other
people don't. To weep and sigh, because I'm
blind? I cannot and I won't."
FANNY CROSBY

"I give thanks unto thee, O Lord, and sing
praises unto thy name."
PSALM 18.49

DAY 166

I am thankful that I am surrounded by a great cloud of witnesses.

DAY 167

"Pride slays thanksgiving, but an humble mind is the soil out of which thanks naturally grows. A proud man is seldom a grateful man, for he never thinks he gets as much as he deserves."
HENRY WARD BEECHER

DAY 168

"To the end that my glory may sing praise to thee, and not be silent. O Lord my God, I will give thanks unto thee for ever."
PSALM 30:12

I am thankful for
contentment.

"The optimist says, the cup is half full. The
pessimist says, the cup is half empty. The child
of God says; My cup runneth over."
ANONYMOUS

"So we thy people and sheep of thy pasture will
give thee thanks for ever: we will show forth thy
praise to all generations."
PSALM 79.13

I am thankful
for true justice.

DAY 173

"Ingratitude denotes spiritual immaturity. Infants do not always appreciate what parents do for them. They have short memories. Their concern is not what you did for me yesterday, but what are you doing for me today. The past is meaningless and so is the future. They live for the present. Those who are mature are deeply appreciative of those who laboured in the past. They recognize those who labour during the present and provide for those who will be labouring in the future."
ANONYMOUS

DAY 174

"Let the heavens rejoice, and let the earth be glad; let the sea roar, and the fulness thereof. Let the field be joyful, and all that is therein: then shall all the trees of the wood rejoice."
PSALM 96:11-12

DAY 175

I am thankful that I can do all things through Christ which strengtheneth me.

DAY 176

"Blessings hemmed with praise
will not unravel."
ANONYMOUS

DAY 177

"Make a joyful noise unto the Lord, all ye lands."
PSALM 100:1

I am thankful for
angels unawares.

DAY 179

"Receive every day as a resurrection from death,
as a new enjoyment of life; meet every rising
sun with such sentiments of God's goodness, as
if you had seen it, and all things, new-created
upon your account: and under the sense of so
great a blessing, let your joyful heart praise and
magnify so good and glorious a Creator."
WILLIAM LAW

DAY 180

"Sing unto him, sing psalms unto him: talk ye
of all his wondrous works."
PSALM 105:2

I am thankful for help when I need it.

"Thanksgiving is the language of heaven, and we had better start to learn it if we are not to be mere dumb aliens there."
ARTHUR JOHN GOSSIP

"Oh that men would praise the Lord for his goodness, and for his wonderful works to the children of men!"
PSALM 107:8

I am thankful for goals to
reach for in life.

"Some people always sigh in thanking God."
SAMUEL JOHNSON

"I thank my God, making mention of thee
always in my prayers."
PHILEMON 1:4

I am thankful for opportunities.

"We prevent God from giving us the great spiritual gifts He has in store for us, because we do not give thanks for daily gifts. We think we dare not be satisfied with the small measure of spiritual knowledge, experience, and love that has been given to us…We pray for the big things and forget to give thanks for the ordinary, small (and yet really not small) gifts. How can God entrust great things to one who will not thankfully receive from Him the little things?"
DIETRICH BONHOEFFER

"Blessed be the God and Father of our Lord Jesus Christ, who hath blessed us with all spiritual blessings in heavenly places in Christ."
EPHESIANS 1:3

I am thankful for the mind to strive to higher heights.

"God be thanked for that good and unspeakable gift. The gift unspeakable: His life, His love, His very self, in Christ Jesus."
MALTBIE D. BABCOCK

"Thou art my God, and I will praise thee: thou art my God, I will exalt thee."
PSALM 118:28

I am thankful that even though
I am not perfect, I am
improving by the grace of God.

"Gratitude is a nice touch of beauty added last
of all to the countenance, giving as classic
beauty, an angelic loveliness, to the character."
THEODORE PARKER

"At midnight I will rise to give thanks unto thee
because of thy righteous judgments."
PSALM 119:62

I am thankful for the whole
armour of God.

"I want to be the most thankful man on the
face of the earth."
BEN FURROW

"O give thanks unto the God of gods: for his
mercy endureth for ever."
PSALM 136:2

I am thankful for those who
endure to the end.

"Gratitude is a fruit of great cultivation; you do
not find it among gross people."
SAMUEL JOHNSON

"I know that the Lord will maintain the cause of
the afflicted, and the right of the poor. Surely
the righteous shall give thanks unto thy name:
the upright shall dwell in thy presence."
PSALM 140:12-13

I am thankful that Jesus is the reason for all seasons.

"To speak gratitude is courteous and pleasant, to enact gratitude is generous and noble, but to live gratitude is to touch Heaven."
JOHANNES A. GAERTNER

"O give thanks unto the God of heaven: for his mercy endureth for ever."
PSALM 136:26

I am thankful that all things
work together for the good.

"Be thankful for what you have; you'll end up
having more. If you concentrate on what you
don't have, you will never, ever have enough."
OPRAH WINFREY

"Praise ye the Lord: for it is good to sing praises
unto our God; for it is pleasant; and praise is
comely."
PSALM 147:1

DAY 208

I am thankful that God loves the entire world and every single person in it.

DAY 209

"Blessed are those that can give without remembering and receive without forgetting."
AUTHOR UNKNOWN

DAY 210

"Sing unto the Lord with thanksgiving; sing praise upon the harp unto our God: Who covereth the heaven with clouds, who prepareth rain for the earth, who maketh grass to grow upon the mountains."
PSALM 147:7-8

I am thankful that God is not a
respector cf persons.

"Difficulties are opportunities to better things;
they are stepping stones to greater experience.
Perhaps someday you will be thankful for some
temporary failure in a particular direction.
When one door closes, another always opens."
AUTHOR UNKNOWN

"For what thanks can we render to God again
for you, for all the joy wherewith we joy for
your sakes before our God."
1 THESSALONIANS 3:9

I am thankful that as a Christian, I am more than a conqueror through Jesus Christ.

"Gratitude is something of which none of us can give too much. For on the smiles, the thanks we give, our little gestures of appreciation, our neighbors build their philosophy of life."
A. J. CRONIN

"To him who alone doeth great wonders: for his mercy endureth for ever."
PSALM 136:4

I am thankful that nothing can separate us from the love of God.

"Develop an attitude of gratitude, and give thanks for everything that happens to you, knowing that every step forward is a step toward achieving something bigger and better than your current situation."
BRIAN TRACY

"Neither filthiness, nor foolish talking, nor jesting, which are not convenient: but rather giving of thanks."
EPHESIANS 5:4

I am thankful that God is in control of my life.

"Every time we remember to say 'thank you', we experience nothing less than heaven on earth."
SARAH BAN BREATHNACH

"We accept it always, and in all places, most noble Felix, with all thankfulness."
ACTS 24:3

I am thankful fcr hard work.

"Feeling grateful or appreciative of someone or
something in your life actually attracts more
of the things that you appreciate and value
into your life."
CHRISTIANE NORTHRUP

"To him that by wisdom made the heavens: for
his mercy endureth for ever."
PSALM 136:5

DAY 226

I am thankful that God hears
and answers prayer.

DAY 227

"Gratitude helps you to grow and expand;
gratitude brings joy and laughter into your life
and into the lives of all those around you."
EILEEN CADDY

DAY 228

"Saying, Amen: Blessing, and glory, and
wisdom, and thanksgiving, and honour, and
power, and might, be unto our God for ever
and ever. Amen."
REVELATION 7:12

I am thankful that Christianity is the simplest, but yet the most profound of all religions.

"He is a wise man who does not grieve for the things which he has not, but rejoices for those which he has."
EPICTETUS

"Because that, when they knew God, they glorified him not as God, neither were thankful; but became vain in their imaginations, and their foolish heart was darkened."
ROMANS 1:21

I am thankful for
blessed assurance.

"If you can't be content with what you have
received, be thankful for what you have
escaped."
AUTHOR UNKNOWN

"And to stand every morning to thank and
praise the LORD, and likewise at even."
1 CHRONICLES 23:30

I am thankful for the opportunity to be a shining light in this dark world.

"If you concentrate on finding whatever is good in every situation, you will discover that your life will suddenly be filled with gratitude, a feeling that nurtures the soul."
RABBI HAROLD KUSHNER

"And Hezekiah appointed the courses of the priests and the Levites after their courses, every man according to his service, the priests and Levites for burnt offerings and for peace offerings, to minister, and to give thanks, and to praise in the gates of the tents of the LORD."
2 CHRONICLES 31:2

I am thankful for humor and laughter.

"If you haven't all the things you want,
be grateful for the things you don't have that
you wouldn't want."
AUTHOR UNKNOWN

"Let all those that seek thee rejoice and be glad
in thee: let such as love thy salvation say
continually, The LORD be magnified."
PSALM 40:16

DAY 241

I am thankful that the direction
of our life is planned by
God's divine will.

DAY 242

"In ordinary life we hardly realize that we
receive a great deal more than we give, and that
it is only with gratitude that life becomes rich."
DIETRICH BONHOEFFER

DAY 243

"Neither say they in their heart, Let us now fear
the LORD our God, that giveth rain, both the
former and the latter, in his season: he reserveth
unto us the appointed weeks of the harvest. Your
iniquities have turned away these things, and your
sins have withholden good things from you."
JEREMIAH 5:24-25

I am thankful that God has the whole world in the palms of His hands.

"It is impossible to feel grateful and depressed in the same moment."
NAOMI WILLIAMS

"And say ye, Save us, O God of our salvation, and gather us together, and deliver us from the heathen, that we may give thanks to thy holy name, and glory in thy praise."
1 CHRONICLES 16:35

I am thankful that life is a
battle, and that because
of the Lord, we are on the
victory side.

"It isn't what you have in your pocket
that makes you thankful, but what you have
in your heart."
AUTHOR UNKNOWN

"Wherefore we receiving a kingdom which
cannot be moved, let us have grace, whereby we
may serve God acceptably with reverence and
godly fear."
HEBREWS 12:28

I am thankful that I can
count my blessings.

"Just a 'thank you' is a mighty powerful prayer.
Says it all."
ROSIE CASH

"Sing unto the LORD with thanksgiving; sing
praise upon the harp unto our God."
PSALM 147:7

I am thankful for what God has said 'No' to.

"Make it a habit to tell people thank you. To express your appreciation, sincerely and without the expectation of anything in return. Truly appreciate those around you, and you'll soon find many others around you. Truly appreciate life, and you'll find that you have more of it."
RALPH MARSTON

"Let us come before his presence with thanksgiving, and make a joyful noise unto him with psalms."
PSALM 95:2

I am thankful that life is not complicated.

"No one who achieves success does so without
the help of others. The wise and confident
acknowledge this help with gratitude."
ALFRED NORTH WHITEHEAD

"I will praise the name of God with a song, and
will magnify him with thanksgiving."
PSALM 69:30

DAY 259

I am thankful for breakthroughs when they are most needed and least expected.

DAY 260

"None is more impoverished than the one who has no gratitude. Gratitude is a currency that we can mint for ourselves, and spend without fear of bankruptcy."
FRED DE WITT VAN AMBURGH

DAY 261

"I will bless the LORD at all times: his praise shall continually be in my mouth."
PSALM 34:1

I am thankful for life here
on earth and the life to come
in Heaven.

"People who live the most fulfilling lives
are the ones who are always rejoicing
at what they have."
RICHARD CARLSON

"Thou hast turned for me my mourning into
dancing: thou hast put off my sackcloth, and
girded me with gladness; To the end that my
glory may sing praise to thee, and not be silent.
O LORD my God, I will give thanks unto
thee for ever."
PSALM 30:11-12

I am thankful for rainbows
even when it doesn't rain.

"So often we dwell on the things that seem
impossible rather than on the things that
are possible. So often we are depressed by
what remains to be done and forget to be
thankful for all that has been done."
MARIAN WRIGHT EDELMAN

"Grant thee according to thine own heart, and
fulfil all thy counsel."
PSALM 20:4

I am thankful that even after
I stopped growing physically, I
continue to grow mentally and
spiritually.

"The grateful mind is constantly fixed upon the
best. Therefore it tends to become the best.
It takes the form or character of the best,
and will receive the best."
WALLACE D. WATTLES

"I will praise thee, O LORD, with my whole
heart; I will shew forth all thy marvellous
works."
PSALM 9:1

DAY 271

I am thankful that burdens are lifted at Calvary.

DAY 272

"The thankful receiver bears a plentiful harvest."
WILLIAM BLAKE

DAY 273

"I will be glad and rejoice in thee: I will sing
praise to thy name, O thou most High."
PSALM 9:2

I am thankful that I do not take
myself too seriously and that
I can laugh at myself.

"God is in control, and therefore in
EVERYTHING I can give thanks - not because
of the situation but because of the One who
directs and rules over it."
KAY ARTHUR

"And the four and twenty elders, which sat
before God on their seats, fell upon their faces,
and worshipped God."
REVELATION 11:16

I am thankful that my life is not my own. It wasn't yesterday, it ain't now, and it never will be.

"There is a calmness to a life lived in Gratitude, a quiet joy."
RALPH H. BLUM

"And all the angels stood round about the throne, and about the elders and the four beasts, and fell before the throne on their faces, and worshipped God."
REVELATION 7:11

I am thankful that good always overcomes evil.

"There is always, always, always something
to be thankful for."
AUTHOR UNKNOWN

"At that time Jesus answered and said, I thank
thee, O Father, Lord of heaven and earth,
because thou hast hid these things from the
wise and prudent, and hast revealed them
unto babes."
MATTHEW 11:25

I am thankful for memories.

DAY 284

"To educate yourself for the feeling of gratitude means to take nothing for granted, but to always seek out and value the kind that will stand behind the action. Nothing that is done for you is a matter of course. Everything originates in a will for the good, which is directed at you. Train yourself never to put off the word or action for the expression of gratitude."
AUTHOR UNKNOWN

DAY 285

"O give thanks to the Lord of lords: for his mercy endureth for ever."
PSALM 136:3

I am thankful that I was made
in the image of God.

"To live a life of gratitude is to open our eyes to
the countless ways in which we are supported by
the world around us. Such a life provides less
space for our suffering because our attention is
more balanced. We are more often occupied with
noticing what we are given, thanking those who
have helped us, and repaying the world in some
concrete way for what we are receiving."
GREGG KRECH

"Therefore will I give thanks unto thee,
O LORD, among the heathen, and sing
praises unto thy name."
PSALM 18:49

I am thankful for the gift
of discernment.

DAY 290

"What if you gave someone a gift, and they
neglected to thank you for it—would you be
likely to give them another? Life is the same
way. In order to attract more of the blessings
that life has to offer, you must truly appreciate
what you already have."
RALPH MARSTON

DAY 291

"And Mattaniah the son of Micha, the son of
Zabdi, the son of Asaph, was the principal to
begin the thanksgiving in prayer."
NEHEMIAH 11:17

I am thankful for forgiveness.

"When I started counting my blessings, my
whole life turned around."
WILLIE NELSON

"And he appointed certain of the Levites to
minister before the ark of the LORD,
and to record, and to thank and praise the
LORD God of Israel."
1 CHRONICLES 16:4

I am thankful for God's hedge of protection that surrounds me.

"You simply will not be the same person two months from now after consciously giving thanks each day for the abundance that exists in your life. And you will have set in motion an ancient spiritual law: the more you have and are grateful for, the more will be given you."
SARAH BAN BREATHNACH

"Then I brought up the princes of Judah upon the wall, and appointed two great companies of them that gave thanks, whereof one went on the right hand upon the wall toward the dung gate."
NEHEMIAH 12:31

I am thankful that small things
matter to God.

"You won't be happy with more until you're
happy with what you've got."
VIKI KING

"Wherefore David blessed the LORD before all
the congregation: and David said, Blessed be
thou, LORD God of Israel our father, for ever
and ever."
1 CHRONICLES 29:10

I am thankful that God continues to bless me so that I can continue to have something to be thankful for.

"Feeling gratitude and not expressing it is like wrapping a present and not giving it."
WILLIAM ARTHUR WARD

"So stood the two companies of them that gave thanks in the house of God, and I, and the half of the rulers with me."
NEHEMIAH 12:40

I am thankful for
joy unspeakable.

"We often take for granted the very things that
most deserve our gratitude."
CYNTHIA OZICK

"But who am I, and what is my people, that we
should be able to offer so willingly after this
sort? for all things come of thee, and of thine
own have we given thee."
1 CHRONICLES 29:14

I am thankful that I am part of God's master plan.

"There is no greater difference between men than between grateful and ungrateful people."
R.H. BLYTH

"Stand up and bless the LORD your God for ever and ever: and blessed be thy glorious name, which is exalted above all blessing and praise."
NEHEMIAH 9:5

I am thankful that people and things in this world may be fleeting, but God and His Word are always the same.

"The greatest saint in the world is not he who prays most or fasts most; it is not he who gives alms, or is most eminent for temperance, chastity or justice. It is he who is most thankful to God."
WILLIAM LAW

"Then on that day David delivered first this psalm to thank the LORD into the hand of Asaph and his brethren."
1 CHRONICLES 16:7

I am thankful for people who care about me enough to tell me when I am wrong.

"There is not a more pleasing exercise of the mind than gratitude. It is accompanied with such an inward satisfaction that the duty is sufficiently rewarded by the performance."
JOSEPH ADDISON

"Give thanks unto the LORD, call upon his name, make known his deeds among the people."
1 CHRONICLES 16:8

I am thankful that there is no success gained without hard work and sacrifice.

"If you want to turn your life around, try thankfulness. It will change your life mightily."
GERALD GOOD

"O give thanks unto the LORD; for he is good; for his mercy endureth for ever."
1 CHRONICLES 16:34

I am thankful for loving parents
who did not give me
everything I wanted, but gave
me what I needed.

"We can only be said to be alive in those
moments when our hearts are conscious
of our treasures."
THORNTON WILDER

"But I will sacrifice unto thee with the voice of
thanksgiving; I will pay that that I have vowed.
Salvation is of the LORD."
JONAH 2:9

DAY 322

I am thankful that the world did not start with me. It is comforting to know that many others have gone before.

DAY 323

"Grace isn't a little prayer you chant before receiving a meal. It's a way to live."
ATTRIBUTED TO JACQUELINE WINSPEAR

DAY 324

"I will praise the LORD according to his righteousness: and will sing praise to the name of the LORD most high."
PSALM 7:17

I am thankful that we live in a colorful and diverse world.

"If a fellow isn't thankful for what he's got,
he isn't likely to be thankful for
what he's going to get."
FRANK A. CLARK

"The LORD is my strength and my shield;
my heart trusted in him, and I am helped:
therefore my heart greatly rejoiceth; and with
my song will I praise him."
PSALM 28:7

I am thankful for the glimpses of the glory of God that we get from nature.

"You say grace before meals. All right. But I say grace before the concert and the opera, and grace before the play and pantomime, and grace before I open a book, and grace before sketching, painting, swimming, fencing, boxing, walking, playing, dancing and grace before I dip the pen in the ink."
G.K. CHESTERTON

"To the end that my glory may sing praise to thee, and not be silent. O LORD my God, I will give thanks unto thee for ever."
PSALM 30:12

I am thankful that God knows
everything and is in control of
the whole world.

"God gave you a gift of 86,400 seconds today.
Have you used one to say 'thank you'?"
WILLIAM A. WARD

"Open to me the gates of righteousness: I will
go into them, and I will praise the LORD."
PSALM 118:19

I am thankful that
everything will work out.

"There is no such thing as gratitude
unexpressed. If it is unexpressed, it is plain,
old-fashioned ingratitude."
ROBERT BRAULT

"I will praise thee: for thou hast heard me,
and art become my salvation."
PSALM 118:21

I am thankful for the unsurpassable, incomprehensible mercy of God.

"Thanksgiving is nothing if not a glad and reverent lifting of the heart to God in honor and praise for His goodness."
ROBERT CASPER LINTNER

"And when he had taken the five loaves and the two fishes, he looked up to heaven, and blessed, and brake the loaves, and gave them to his disciples to set before them; and the two fishes divided he among them all."
MARK 6:41

I am thankful that when I pray,
I don't bring God to my point
of view, but He brings me to
His point of view.

"There is no greater prayer than one of sincere
heartfelt love, appreciation, and gratitude."
JACK CANFIELD

"Let the word of Christ dwell in you richly
in all wisdom; teaching and admonishing
one another in psalms and hymns
and spiritual songs, singing with grace
in your hearts to the Lord."
COLOSSIANS 3:16

I am thankful that God continues to bless millions of people with the same blessings.

DAY 344

"Got no check books, got no banks. Still I'd like to express my thanks—I got the sun in the morning and the moon at night."
IRVING BERLIN

DAY 345

"Oh how great is thy goodness, which thou hast laid up for them that fear thee; which thou hast wrought for them that trust in thee before the sons of men!"
PSALM 31:19

I am thankful that the truth
always sets us free.

"O Lord that lends me life,
Lend me a heart replete with thankfulness."
WILLIAM SHAKESPEARE

"They shall abundantly utter the memory
of thy great goodness, and shall sing of
thy righteousness."
PSALM 145:7

I am thankful for the ability to live life in a simple way.

"If I have enjoyed the hospitality of the Host of this universe, Who daily spreads a table in my sight, surely I cannot do less than acknowledge my dependence."
G.A. JOHNSTON ROSS

"Let all those that seek thee rejoice and be glad in thee: and let such as love thy salvation say continually, Let God be magnified."
PSALM 70:4

I am thankful for hope.

"Perhaps it takes a purer faith to praise God for
unrealized blessings than for those we once
enjoyed or those we enjoy now."
A. W. Tozer

"Save us, O LORD our God, and gather us from
among the heathen, to give thanks unto thy
holy name, and to triumph in thy praise."
Psalm 106:47

I am thankful for the peace
that comes with surrendering
my will to God's will.

"Thanksgiving is possible only for those who
take time to remember; no one can give thanks
who has a short memory."
AUTHOR UNKNOWN

"Oh that men would praise the LORD for his
goodness, and for his wonderful works to the
children of men!"
PSALMS 107:31

DAY 358

I am thankful for the fruits of the Spirit.

DAY 359

"I thank God for my handicaps, for,
through them, I have found myself,
my work, and my God."
HELEN KELLER

DAY 360

"Glory ye in his holy name: let the heart of them
rejoice that seek the Lord."
PSALMS 105:3

I am thankful for
God's Holy Word.

"If you suffer, thank God!
It is a sure sign that you are alive."
ELBERT HUBBARD

"So we thy people and sheep of thy pasture will
give thee thanks for ever: we will shew forth thy
praise to all generations."
PSALMS 79.13

I am thankful that I have something to be thankful for.

"Thank God for clothes to wear;
For food to eat;
For people who care;
And for money under the car seat."
DANIEL WHYTE III

"Whoso offereth praise glorifieth me: and to
him that ordereth his conversation aright will I
shew the salvation of God."
PSALMS 50:23

THE ULTIMATE THANKS

After reading this book, you may still feel as though you have nothing for which to be thankful, or at least to be thankful for every day. But that is not the case. Even if you can't find one thing of your own to be thankful for everyday, I am about to tell you of something you can be thankful for everyday, all day. Over two thousand years ago, Jesus Christ died on the cross for your sins, my sins, and the sins of the entire world. He took our shame upon Himself so that we could have the hope of eternal life. If you do not know Jesus Christ, please read the following. After you accept Him into your heart, He will not only make all the difference in your life, but you will be forever thankful for new life in Jesus:

1. Accept the truth that God loves you so much that He sent His only Son, Jesus Christ, to die on Calvary and pay for your sins. *"For God so loved the world, that He gave His only begotten Son, that whosoever believeth in Him should not perish, but have everlasting life."* (Jesus Christ, John 3:16).

2. Accept the truth that you are a sinner, who has broken God's laws. Romans 3: 10, 23 says *"As it is written, There is none righteous, no, not one..."* *"For all have sinned, and come short of the glory of God."*

3. Accept the truth that there is a price for sin and that you are on your way to an eternal hell. The Bible says in Romans 6:23: *"For the wages of sin is death..."* Revelation 21:8 says, *"But the fearful, and unbelieving, and the abominable, and murderers, and whoremongers and sorcerers, and idolaters, and all liars, shall have their part in the lake which burneth with fire and brimstone: which is the second death."*

4. Accept the truth that Jesus is your only way to be saved from eternal punishment. *"Neither is there salvation in any other: for there is none other name under heaven given among men, whereby we must be saved"* (Acts 4:12).

5. Confess the truth that Jesus Christ is Lord, and believe in your heart that Jesus Christ died for

you, was buried and rose again to save you. The Bible states in Romans 10:9, 13: *"That if thou shalt confess with thy mouth the Lord Jesus, and shalt believe in thine heart that God hath raised him from the dead, thou shalt be saved." "For whosoever shall call upon the name of the Lord shall be saved."*

If you believe with all of your heart that Jesus Christ loves you so much that He died for you, was buried, and rose on the third day, please pray this prayer:

Lord Jesus, I know that I am a sinner, deserving of hell. I do not want to go to hell, but rather, I want to live with you throughout eternity. Lord, I now believe with all of my heart that Jesus Christ died for me, was buried, and rose by the power of God. I confess you as my Lord and Saviour, right now. Please come into my heart and save my soul, this very moment. In Jesus Christ's precious name. Amen!